IMAGES OF LONDON

WOMEN AT WORK
ON LONDON's TRANSPORT
1905-1978

IMAGES OF LONDON

WOMEN AT WORK
ON LONDON's TRANSPORT
1905-1978

ANNA ROTONDARO

TEMPUS

Frontispiece: Metropolitan Railway guards at Neasden station, *c*.1915.

First published 2004

Tempus Publishing Limited
The Mill, Brimscombe Port,
Stroud, Gloucestershire, GL5 2QG
www.tempus-publishing.com

British Library Cataloguing in Publication Data.
A catalogue record for this book is available from the British Library.

ISBN 0 7524 3265 6

Typesetting and origination by Tempus Publishing Limited.
Printed in Great Britain.

Contents

Acknowledgements

I would like to the following at London's Transport Museum for their invaluable advice, assistance and time throughout the production of this book: David Bownes, Oliver Green, Hugh Robertson, Bryan Wills, Mike Ashworth and my colleagues Samantha, Simon, Martin and Stawell in the photographic library.

Thanks are also due to my mother Ann, sister Frances, and to Stephen and John for all of their encouragement and support during this project.

Introduction

The rapid development of pubic transport in nineteenth century London provided a
wealth of jobs for men operating and maintaining horse buses and trams and on the
railways, but little in the way of opportunities for women. It was not until the outbreak
of the First World War that the process of establishing women in the transport
workplace began. The initial effects of war put a huge strain on London's transport
systems. The mobilization of men called away to fight resulted in vast reductions of staff
across the industry. It fast became apparent that alternative sources of labour were
needed, and with great reluctance the trade unions and male-dominated management
finally conceded to allow women to work in what were then traditionally male roles.

When Maida Vale Underground station opened on 6 June 1915, it was staffed
entirely by women. The London General Omnibus Company (LGOC), although at
first hesitant, began to employ women in 1916. Pay for a woman was considered
generous at the time but was not equal to that of the men whom they replaced. The
T.O.T (Tram, Omnibus and Train) War Record reported in December 1919 that 5,551
women were employed during the First World War by the Underground Companies,
working in a variety of positions on both the railways and the buses. However, it was
understood that the replacement of men during the war would only ever be a
temporary measure. When the war ended in 1918 women returned to their previous
work and way of life, and would not reappear as conductors on London's buses for
another twenty-one years.

During the Second World War women were called upon again to fill employment;
however, this time it was on a much larger scale. As staff shortages became acute, it was
necessary to employ women in more diverse types of work in depots and engineering
departments. The driving of vehicles still remained a 'reserved occupation' for men
only, although some women were allowed to drive empty vehicles at bus depots and to
and from garages.

The numbers of women employed by London Transport at this time rose to almost
20,000. The importance of the work undertaken by the women was reflected in the
appointment of 'Women Welfare Officers' and the creation of nursery facilities for
working mothers, to ensure the needs of staff were taken care of at every opportunity.

Unlike the First World War, this time when the war ended a change in London Transport policy meant that many women were allowed to continue in the jobs they had carried out so proficiently.

The post-war period saw a decline in the wages offered to transport staff compared to that of other industries, resulting in severe staff shortages. An extensive recruitment campaign targeted women from Britain and overseas to work as bus conductors, station staff and canteen assistants.

The Equal Opportunities Act (1974) and Equal Pay Act (1975) finally granted women equal rights and working conditions. London Transport's first woman bus driver, Jill Viner, was appointed in 1974, shortly followed by Hannah Dadds, the first female Underground train driver. Soon vacancies were filled in mechanics and engineering grades and the first female bus mechanic, Helen Clifford, qualified in 1984.

This collection of photographs has been selected from the archives of London's Transport Museum and follows the development of women working in London's transport industry or services. The earliest depicts a typist employed by the District Railway in 1905, and the collection finishes with the first women bus and tube drivers, who were employed in the mid-1970s. Wherever possible, contemporary photographs have been used, the majority of which were commissioned to document the remarkable war work undertaken by women during the First and Second World Wars. Most of the photographs were taken by Topical Press photographic agency, and were commissioned by the Underground Electric Railways Company of London (UERL) from 1906 for company records and publicity. When London Transport took over in 1933 it continued this tradition, and every activity was photographed from technical operations to publicity material. Many of the photographs featured in this book were specifically commissioned to illustrate articles in staff magazines, while most of the post-war portraits of conductors were taken for use in recruitment poster campaigns.

The accompanying text and captions can only provide an overview of the history of women at work in London's Transport services. The following publications provided an invaluable source of information throughout the preparation of this book: *Pennyfare*, the London Transport staff magazine from 1933 (originally titled *T.O.T Staff Magazine* after the Train, Omnibus Tram employees' mutual aid fund); *London Transport Magazine* (copies dating from 1947–1973); and issues of *LT News* (January 1977–December 1978), which are held in the museum library.

Those interested in learning more about the subject are recommended to read *The Moving Metropolis: A History of London's Transport since 1800*, edited by Sheila Taylor (2001); *A Journey through Time: London Transport Photographs 1880 to 1965*, Sheila Taylor (1992); *Rails through the Clay: A History of London's Tube Railways*, Desmond F. Croome and Alan A. Jackson (1993). *A History of London Transport: Volume Two – The Twentieth Century to 1970*, T.C. Barker and Michael Robbins (1974); and *London Transport at War 1939–1945*, Charles Graves (1974).

Copies of most prints reproduced in this publication may be purchased by writing to the address below and quoting the reference number in square brackets at the end of each caption. Personal visits to view the photographic collection, which covers all aspects of London's public transport, can be made by appointment.

Anna Rotondaro, Curator (Multi-media collections)
The Photo Library, London's Transport Museum, Covent Garden, WC2E 7BB
www.ltmuseum.co.uk
Tel: 0207 379 6344

one

1905–1918

Left and below: These are the earliest photographs in the museum collection, featuring a female member of staff working at Ealing Common Depot, District Railway, 1905. Miss Armstrong was the first typist to be employed at the new Depot. In the view of the office, Miss Armstrong can be seen on the far left. [2003/8696], [2003/8708]

A ticket collector checks a ticket at the newly opened Maida Vale Underground station, Bakerloo line, 1915. The Underground Group was the first to employ 'women substitutes' during the First World War. When the new station at Maida Vale opened on 6 June 1915, it was the first to be staffed entirely by women: two ticket collectors, two porters, two booking clerks and two relief ticket-collector booking clerks. The *Railway Gazette* expressed its guarded approval in an article about the women, stating it was 'preferable to employing hobbledehoys'. (Hobbledehoys are clumsy or awkward youths.) [1998/39279]

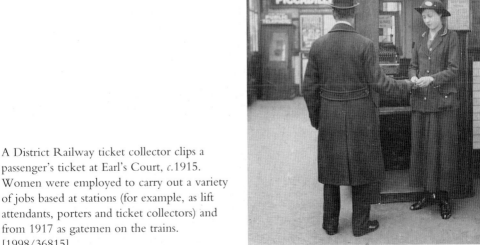

A District Railway ticket collector clips a passenger's ticket at Earl's Court, *c.*1915. Women were employed to carry out a variety of jobs based at stations (for example, as lift attendants, porters and ticket collectors) and from 1917 as gatemen on the trains. [1998/36815]

A London Electric Railway lift attendant holding the gate to a lift open, around 1915. [1998/85033]

A District Railway guard on the platform of Earl's Court Underground station. [1998/36816]

Right: A porter poses next to the first-class compartment of a District Railway train, *c.*1915. [1998/52486]

Below: A Bakerloo line 'gateman' poses at Watford Junction station, *c.*1917. It was the duty of the 'gateman' to open the doors, having announced the name of the station upon the train's arrival, and to open and close the gates when passengers were boarding and leaving the train. Although women replaced 'gatemen' on trains, men remained as front and rear guards. [1998/36852]

Two District Railway women pose in uniform in front of semaphore signals on the platform of West Kensington station, c.1915. [1998/36843]

A group of Metropolitan Railway guards at Neasden station, c.1915. Hand lamps and flags were used for signalling. [1998/84356]

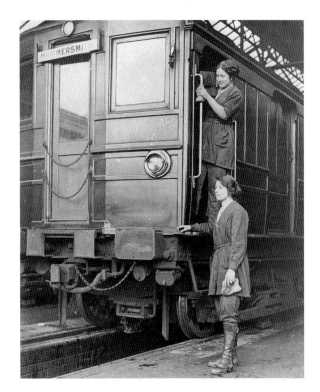

Right: Two Metropolitan Railway cleaners working at Hammersmith Depot, Hammersmith & City Railway, *c.*1915. Women were employed to carry out a number of general maintenance jobs including painting, bill posting and general cleaning duties. [2002/9493]

Below: A group of Underground maintenance workers pose for the camera, *c.*1917. [1998/62230]

A Metropolitan Railway guard waves a flag signalling the departure of the train from the platform at Neasden station, 1917. By the end of that year, the Metropolitan Railway had 522 female staff. [1998/84028]

A Metropolitan Railway guard fills in a logbook in the station ticket office or storeroom, in around 1917. [1998/83581]

Above and right: Metropolitan Railway guard Eva Carver poses both in her everyday attire and whilst on duty as a station guard at Hammersmith, Metropolitan and Great Western Railways station, *c.*1917. The photographs were used in an article entitled 'How a woman helps' in *Great Western Railway* magazine, about female conductors working on the Metropolitan Railway. [2004/2912], [2004/2926], [2004/2929]

Underground staff in the mess room dining area of Earl's Court station, *c.*1914. [1998/47076]

Opposite, above and below: Staff members relax in the Brompton Road staff club for women, around 1918. From May 1918, part of the street-level building of the station was used to house a women's institute and club for Underground employees. [1998/83578], [1998/53884]

LONDON GENERAL OMNIBUS COMPANY, L^{TD.}

WANTED

WOMEN
CONDUCTORS

HEIGHT MUST NOT BE
LESS THAN 5 FEET
AGE BETWEEN
21 AND 35

APPLY BETWEEN 10.0 A.M. AND 1.0 P.M.
ON WEEKDAYS (SATURDAYS EXCEPTED)

THE SUPERINTENDENT OF EMPLOYMENT,
L.G.O. CO'S. TRAINING SCHOOL,
MILMAN'S STREET,
S.W.

THE DANGERFIELD PRINTING COMPANY, LIMITED, LONDON

A queue of women applicants line up to be interviewed for the position of conductor with the London General Omnibus Company (LGOC), in around 1916. Figures collated that year reported that 1,702 women had joined the LGOC as conductors by the end of 1916. Analysis of applicants' previous employment found that the women had been waitresses, shop assistants, clerks, cashiers, tailoresses and dressmakers, but most had previously worked as domestic servants. [1998/48277]

Opposite: 'Wanted Women Conductors', November 1916. The London General Omnibus Company, although reluctantly at first, considered employing women conductors in 1915. This recruitment poster in an attempt to specifically attract female applicants to roles previously held by men. [2003/24157]

Above and below: Candidates are interviewed at LGOC premises, *c.*1915. [1998/65935], [1998/65217]

Above and below: Trainees learn how to deal with passengers and also the bus routes on which they will eventually work, *c.*1915. New recruits were taught at the LGOC's training school for conductors and drivers at Milman Street in Chelsea. [1998/37396], [2003/7630]

The conductors relax with tea at the end of the day. [1998/36757]

Opposite, above and below: Trainees learn about fare stages and the ticketing system, around 1915. [1998/36754], [1998/65940]

Above: LGOC conductors or 'Clippies' were issued with a free uniform once training had been completed. The navy blue serge uniform comprised a calf-length skirt and jacket with white piping, and a moulded felt hat with a 'General' badge. [1998/85837]

Opposite, above and below: Recruits take a lesson outside the classroom at Milman Street and inspect a B-type motorbus on which they will eventually work. [1998/36015], [1998/42750]

An LGOC conductor poses in winter uniform with a long overcoat, *c.*1916. She also wears an enamel licence badge, Bell Punch and leather cash bag, and is carrying her wooden ticket rack. [1998/57474]

A white lighter weight jacket, known as a 'dust coat', and a straw hat was provided for the summer months, *c.*1916. [1998/62180]

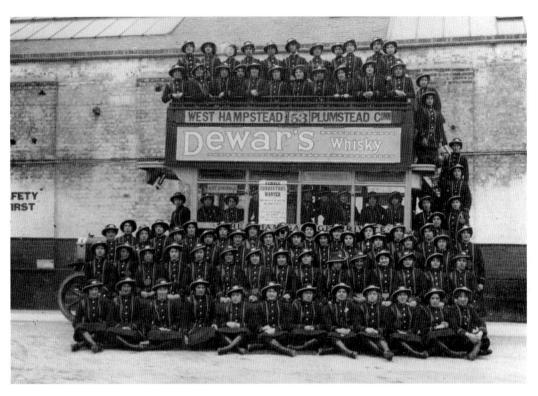

Above and below: Once training was complete, the newly qualified conductors attended a passing out parade. These pictures are from around 1916–1918. [1998/65223], [1998/84852]

Mrs G. Duncan, the very first woman conductor in London, started work on a No.37 Tilling's bus on 1 November 1915. The LGOC followed, employing women conductors in 1916. By the end of 1917, 522 women had been employed by the LGOC in a variety of jobs. [1998/39105]

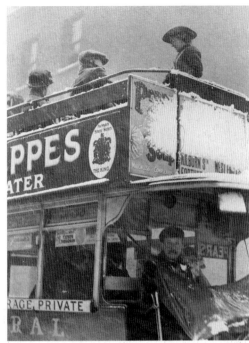

Above and right: LGOC bus conductors on service, *c.*1916–1919. Once training was complete, conductors worked on a weekly shift rota. The work was not easy and not without its dangers. Clippies worked an early shift one week, relief another, then ended on a late shift. The early shift began at 6 a.m. and all shifts lasted ten hours, with a six-day working week. [1998/48735], [1998/39935], [1998/25242]

Left, below and opposite: Women were employed by the LGOC for a range of duties at garages and engineering works. They worked as storekeepers in the fitting shops of the engineering works, on general maintenance of the buses and cleaning. Some were even involved in overhauling the B-type bus chassis. These pictures date from around 1916–1919. [1998/84038], [1998/83598], [1998/84037]

A London County Council Tramways conductor in summer uniform, *c.*1915–1919. The Metropolitan Police agreed to grant licenses to women conductors in October 1915. The first LCCT women conductors began work on single-deck tramcars on 30 November. By the end of August 1916, women had progressed to working on double-deck trailer cars. The LCCT issued a uniform that consisted of a long navy blue linen jacket and ankle-length skirt, with a 'panama'-style hat, displaying an LCC button-style cap badge. A lighter weight dustcoat was issued for the summer months. Ankle-height boots and leather gaiters were worn to protect the women from knocks and bumps when riding the tram. A number of notices were issued by the chief officer of the LCCT to all depots and car sheds to remind the women that, 'the uniform must be worn exactly as supplied', as it had been observed that 'lace and other fancy collars' were being worn. [1985/43]

Tram driver Mr Walter Barham poses at the controls with colleagues, including a woman conductor at London County Council Tramways' Camberwell Depot, in around 1917. [2004/3378]

Miss Florrie Wilson poses in London County Council Tramways' uniform and a non-regulation hat. Miss Wilson was employed by the LCCT from 16 December 1915 to 6 August 1919. On 8 June 1916 the chief officer of the LCCT issued an instruction to all lady conductors that short hat pins or protective stoppers for longer pins should be used to secure their hats whilst working. This precautionary measure was to guard against any personal injury or 'damage to clothing' claims made by passengers caused by the long hatpins worn by the conductors, which were fashionable at the time. [1998/83580]

Studio portrait of Mrs Pester, née Eliza Bulpritt, who worked as a Leyton District Council Tramways conductor during the First World War. The Leyton uniform consisted of a blue serge jacket and skirt with the conductor's grade and 'LCCT' initials embroidered on to the collar of the jacket. [1985/49]

Above: Metropolitan Electric Tramways conductors, 1917–1919. The women wear the standard issue MET uniform, consisting of a dark grey jacket and skirt (edged with black leather about the cuffs and hems), a grey straw hat and black leather calf-length boots with gaiters. Women enlisted at Manor House offices and underwent a basic medical examination. MET conductors worked a ten-hour day, six days a week, with one free day a week. Pay was £1 10s per week during training and rose to around £2 per week once training had been completed. In total, around 160 female conductors were employed by the company during the First World War. [1998/83577]

Opposite: 'Hampstead Heath', by Nancy Smith, 1915. In 1908, Frank Pick was given responsibility for the Underground Group's publicity, including posters, press advertisements and guidebooks, in an attempt to encourage off-peak travel, especially on public holidays and to countryside destinations. The Underground became an art patron to both established and unknown artists alike. This is one of the earliest posters in the museum collection to have been designed by a female artist. [1983/4/639]

HAMPSTEAD HEATH

THE NEAREST POINT TO LONDON
FOR FUN AND FRESH AIR

BY

'Take Your Family to…
August Bank Holiday', by
Agnes Richardson, 1915.
During the First World
War, the Underground
Group continued to
promote pleasure trips to the
country. Posters depicting
the countryside were also
sent to troops serving
overseas by the UERL
(Underground Electric
Railways company of
London) to decorate huts
and billers with reminders of
home. [2000/9403]

two

1919–1938

LAST WOMAN CONDUCTOR LEFT
19th NOVEMBER 1919.

GENERAL

LONDON GENERAL OMNIBUS Co LTD

Certificate of Service
rendered during the Great War
1914 — 1919.

This is to Certify that

Miss E Bulfield

was employed by The London General Omnibus Co Ltd

as *Conductor*

from *13 3 1916* to *18 - 11 - 1919*

Operating Manager.

Above: LGOC certificate of 'service rendered during the Great War'. During Miss Bulfield's service (1916–1919), it was estimated she had travelled around 70,000 miles. The conductors were all issued with commemorative certificates and photographs to mark their service with the company. [2001/53590]

Opposite: Ellen Bulfield, the last woman bus conductor employed by the London General Omnibus Company, ceremonially hands her position over to a male colleague almost a year after the end of the war. The trade unions were assured that the employment of women as conductors on buses during the First World War would only ever be a temporary measure. The LGOC fulfilled its national promise to the discharged soldiers, and all jobs were kept open to those who returned from the war. [2001/56628]

London Underground Railways
and
London
General Omnibus Company, Ltd.

SOUVENIR
PROGRAMME

———— of the ————

Farewell Social Gathering

of Past and Present Women War Workers
on the London Underground Railways
and London General Omnibus
Company, Ltd., held at the

PEOPLE'S PALACE, MILE END
On TUESDAY, OCTOBER 21, 1919

PRESENTATION OF CERTIFICATES OF SERVICE

Chairman · H. E. BLAIN, Esq.
Organist · J. A. MEALE, Esq.

M.C.'s of the Dance:
Mr. F. COLLIER, Mr. J. C. SEAGER.
M.C.'s of the Whist Drive:
Mr. R. A. BUNN, Mr. F. TURNER.
Hon. Secretary · · Miss A. MONKS.

Souvenir programme of the 'Farewell Social Gathering of Past and Present Women War Workers', Tuesday 21 October 1919. Those who worked for London Underground Railways and the London General Omnibus Company during the First World War were invited to attend an event at the People's Palace on the Mile End Road in London. [2001/53591]

Above and below: The Farewell Social Gathering, October 1919. Certificates of service were presented and refreshments were given. Entertainments in the form of a dance and whist drive were provided in recognition of all the efforts made by the women during the war. [1998/83605], [1998/43329]

T.O.T (Train, Omnibus and Tram) Victory Day celebrations, 30 June 1919. The T.O.T Mutual Aid fund was founded in the first month of the war. All employees, regardless of their position, contributed a weekly subscription fee depending on their means. Every penny that was contributed was matched in sum by the T.O.T. The 'Truth T.O.T War Record' reported that over £250,000 was paid to the dependants of the companies during the First World War. The fund was used to pay for social gatherings and outings for the wives and children of the soldiers called to war. Activities included trips to the country and Christmas entertainments. [1998/36862]

'From Country to the Heart of Town', a poster by Dora M. Batty, 1925. During the 1920s and '30s Dora Batty was the most prolific female poster artist for the Underground, producing at least sixty works during this period. She was also a talented dress designer and became Head of the Textiles Department of the LCC's Central School of Arts and Crafts (now Central St Martin's College of Art and Design). [1983/4/1857]

A press advertisement published in the *London's Suburbs* series, 'Why not live at Stanmore?' by Christine H. Jackson, 1929. This is an example of an advertisement designed directly to appeal to women, promoting lifestyle choices and encouraging a move out of the city into the country. [1998/99361]

Three telephonists work the switchboard at the telephone exchange at Leicester Square Underground station, *c*.1920. The diversity of work offered to women lessened after the men returned from war. [1998/48393]

Rows of typists at work in the 'central typing office' at 55 Broadway, London Underground's then new headquarters, 21 April 1931. [1999/10361]

Cashiers check and analyse bus conductors' cash total sheets in the Traffic Audit Department, 55 Broadway, October 1933. [1998/48713]

First prize winners of the 'bonny baby' show competition at the T.O.T (Train, Omnibus and Tram) Sports Gala at Chiswick Works sports ground, 25 July 1931. London Underground and later London Transport organised a variety of annual sports days, recreational activities and athletics associations for its staff. [2004/4906]

The women's 'egg and spoon' race in progress at the T.O.T (Train, Omnibus and Tram) sports gala at Chiswick Works sports ground, 25 July 1932. [1999/10888]

A 'punch girl' reseals a Bell Punch ticket machine, Chiswick Works ticket office, 1927. Women were in the majority at the ticket office, where tickets were produced, checked, sorted and distributed. The number and value of the tickets issued (and any suspicion of fraud by the conductors) could be checked by counting the 'confetti' retained in the Bell Punch. 'A trick of nature has destined women for this job' commented *London Transport Magazine*, 'unlike men, they are practically never colour blind.' [1999/7726]

Workers in the 'tracing section' of the London Transport Chief Engineer's drawing office work on plans and drawings, 55 Broadway, 23 August 1938. [1998/48753]

Winding armature coils from tram motors at Charlton Works, 1932. Women were considered particularly adept at this type of intricate work, as seen here at the central repair works for the London County Council. [1998/50465]

Chiswick Bus Works canteen staff serve and prepare food, January 1935. Soon after this photograph was taken, the canteen at Chiswick was rebuilt in order to accommodate greatly increased staff numbers. [1998/20551]

Acton Railway Works canteen staff line up in the servery area, ready to serve workers hot and cold meals and refreshments, June 1938. This is an example of a newly refurbished canteen. Canteen staff continually had to adapt to changes and improvements in the modernisation of the service. [1998/47209]

three

1939–1949

Left: 'Enjoy your War Work', 1941, featuring bus conductor Mabel Edna Notley (Conductor Notley 5109), who worked at Leatherhead Country Bus Garage on routes 406, 408 and 418 around Epsom. Miss Notley was interviewed for staff magazine *Pennyfare* regarding her work in May 1941. Before the war, she worked in the lace department of Bentall's department store in Kingston, but applied for the position as she felt she should be 'going to it', as was expected of everyone.

Above: Twins Rosemary and Dale Barker, receiving training from an instructor, 12 April 1944. Initial classroom training lasted between three and six days. Training for conductors assigned to work on trams or trolleybuses lasted up to six days, as the ticketing system for these modes was more complex. The women finally underwent a period of 'road training' on service vehicles with qualified male conductors, which usually lasted between seven and eleven days. After training an examination was taken at the training centre. [1998/53870]

Opposite below: Bus conductors chosen to take part in a *Daily Express* pageant pose at Hammersmith Garage, 23 April 1942. The women are, from left to right: Mrs Lily Hiatt (Victoria Garage), Mrs Rosina Webb (Camberwell Garage), Mrs Dorothy Jacobs (Willesden Garage), Mrs Agnes Page (Camberwell Garage), Mrs Ivy Godson (Camberwell Garage), and Mrs Elsie Hardy (Twickenham Garage). [1998/35997]

Left: Mrs Marjorie Elizabeth Pearman, bus conductor from Middle Row Garage, assists a passenger, June 1943. New conductors were regarded as being on probation for the first three months of their service and were interviewed at the end of each month. The divisional superintendent carried out a final interview and decided whether or not a candidate was taken on as permanent staff. [1998/28240]

Above: Bexleyheath trolleybus depot staff help to clear wreckage caused by a 'V1' flying bomb, 29 June 1944. Staff often had to deal with the aftermath of damage to buildings and vehicles. The vulnerability of the trolleybus system from air-raid attack soon became apparent after an attack in New Malden on 16 August 1940. If overhead wiring became damaged, a whole section of the network became affected. Maintenance crews worked quickly to replace damaged overhead wiring and traction poles. The average time taken to reinstate the trolleybus service was a mere four hours. [1998/35205]

Opposite below: A conductor issues tickets to passengers on the lower deck of SA-type trolleybus No.1722, November 1941. Originally, conductors were issued with a uniform that comprised a tunic, divided skirt, dustcoat and cap, that was to serve both the summer and winter months. After complaints that the issue was insufficient – too cold for the winter and too warm for the summer months – the uniform was adapted and a light dustcoat for the summer and heavy overcoat for winter were provided. Women soon favoured wearing trousers instead of skirts to work. A London Transport public relations document dated 1943 suggested 'opinion may have been influenced by the difficulty in obtaining adequate supplies of stockings'. [1998/54579]

Mrs Olive White, a canteen assistant at Nunhead Bus Garage, talks to a member of staff, July 1944. Mrs White, a widow of a tram conductor, worked at the garage for four years through some of the worst air raids of the Second World War. Although her home was blasted three times, she was absent only once from work throughout this period. [1998/46962]

A member of canteen staff from Old Ford Bus Garage works at an emergency oven, following bomb damage to the premises, 15 December 1941. London Transport staff dealt with such incidents quickly and with initiative to provide a continuous service for employees, ensuring staff received their daily square meals. [1998/35838]

Conductors from Plumstead Garage relax in an ARP (air–raid precautions) rest room. Special 'women only' accommodation was provided for use, especially during night air raids. The trainees met with a women's 'welfare supervisor', who could advise on any personal issues or domestic problems. Supervisors for all modes of transport (bus, tram, trolleybus and rail) regularly toured the garages and stations. [1998/36854]

Effra Road Ticket Printing Works staff knit 'comforts' for servicemen as part of the London Transport WARCO (War Comforts Fund Association) scheme, 19 January 1940. Members knitted approximately 211,500 woollen garments for the forces in total. By the end of the Second World War, WARCO had also awarded £88,794 for more than 14,000 cases of air raid and other distress. [1998/23471]

Above: Chiswick Bus Works staff bail used bus destination blinds, 15 April 1943. Many uses were found for the old blinds to aid the war effort. An article in *Woman* magazine in 1943 reported some of the blinds were turned into mats for use under the bus drivers' feet, as rubber was unobtainable during the war years. [1998/47749]

Above: Electrician's mate, Mrs M. Gladman, works with an electrician at Charlton Tram and Trolleybus Works, 12 May 1942. Women usually started working in the Engineers Department as cleaners or labourers' assistants. If they proved successful, they were offered the opportunity to specialise in a particular branch of work as mechanical or electrical fitters assistants and machine women. [1998/35962]

Right: Progress assistant Mrs E. Munro takes inventory at Charlton Tram and Trolleybus Works, 12 May 1942. [1998/35963]

Opposite below: Mrs Simpson works on a bus chassis in Chiswick Bus Works, 23 July 1941. London Transport stopped building new buses here during the war. As the shortage of materials and spare parts became acute, women were trained to give older buses a complete overhaul, which included cleaning and repairing the bus chassis. [1998/35910]

Left: Fitter Mrs L. Brown at work in the Charlton Tram and Trolleybus Works, 12 May 1942. [1998/35965]

Below: Capstan lathe operator Miss G. Meyer, Charlton Tram and Trolleybus Works, 12 May 1942. [1998/35966]

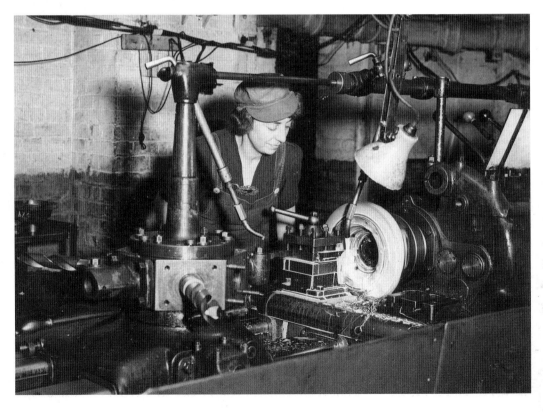

Right: Metal cutter Miss E. Reeves uses an oxy-acetylene torch to cut sheet metal at Charlton Tram and Trolleybus Works, 12 May 1942. [1998/35960]

Below: Miss N. Palmer operates a milling lathe at Charlton Tram and Trolleybus Works, 12 May 1942. [1998/35956]

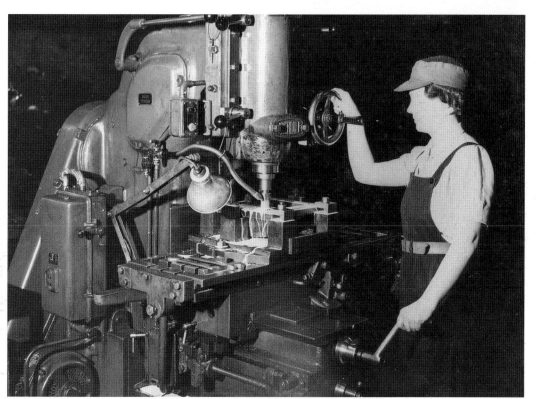

Above and opposite, above: An instructor gives a demonstration of the signalling system with the aid of a model railway, and trainees attend a lecture on the effects of a poison gas attack at Lambeth North Training School, November 1942. Classroom training for porters lasted for three days followed by a further three days of practical training under supervision. [1998/23783], 1998/38578]

Right: 'A Woman's Job In War', 1941. Just as in the First World War, women were again called to work when 3,481 male members of the Underground staff enlisted to fight in the Second World War. [1983/4/5438]

Above and below: Trainee porters learn about the platform signalling system and hand-signal operation at Lambeth North Training School, November 1942. [1998/23792], [1998/23483]

A porter (yet to be issued with a full uniform) signals using a flag on the platform of Chancery Lane station, 18 September 1940. The photograph was taken on the day the first group of female porters went on duty at Underground stations, following three days' instruction at Lambeth North Training School Training School. [1998/84489]

Porter Mrs Clara Taverna shouts 'Mind the doors' to passengers through a megaphone nicknamed 'Meg', Piccadilly Circus station, 19 March 1941. The role of a porter was varied and ranged from dealing with public enquiries to working behind the scenes, ensuring the Underground system ran smoothly on a daily basis. [1998/47838]

Left and below: Porter Mrs Gibbs operates a loudspeaker and performs hand signals on the platforms of Baker Street station, 30 April 1942. [1998/35825], [1998/35878]

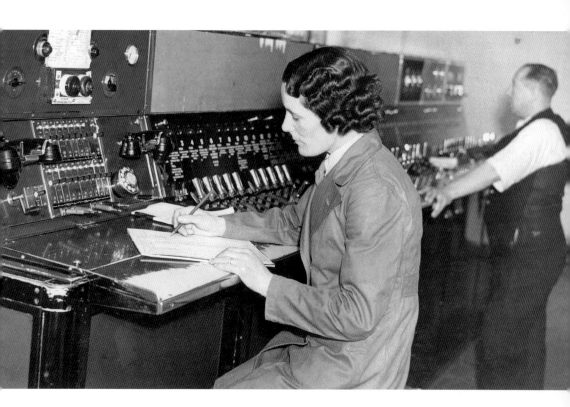

Above: Porter Mrs Lowrey takes on the role of a 'Box boy' in the signal box at Baker Street station, 30 November 1942. [1998/68925]

Right: A porter cleans a sign in Charing Cross Underground station, 23 February 1943. [1998/23476]

Left: Goods porters Miss Gaygill and Mrs Hodgkins load crates on to a train, Baker Street station, 30 April 1942. Work often involved lifting and carrying heavy items requiring the women to be fit. [1998/35795]

Below: Interior of a wartime tube car with anti-blast netting, and 'Caledonian' seating fabric designed by Marion Dorn, 7 March 1941. Dorn was a prolific textile designer who exhibited in a variety of London galleries and European Arts and Crafts Exhibitions throughout the 1920s and '30s . In 1936 she was commissioned to design seating 'moquettes' for use on London Transport vehicles by Christian Barman, the Publicity Officer. [1998/36489]

Right and below: Sisters Mrs Fowkes and Mrs Smith at work in the booking offices at Mansion House and West Brompton Underground stations, 1 March 1944. Training for booking clerks lasted a month, a week at a training school followed by three weeks based in a station. Women over the age of thirty usually took the position of a booking clerk; a few had previously been employed during the First World War. [1998/23487], [1998/23479]

Above: The 'Tube Refreshments Special' being loaded at Wood Lane Underground station, December 1940. When the German bombers flew over London in the first mass raid on the night of 7 September 1940, people sought unofficial shelter underground as they had during the First World War. London Transport was soon forced to organise and regulate shelter arrangements on the overcrowded deep platforms. Food and refreshments were distributed to the stations every night by special trains, and handed out to the shelterers. [1998/84948]

Above: Holland Park Underground station, December 1940. LT staff prepare to serve refreshments to the shelterers. [1998/36094]

Right: St James's Park Underground station, December 1940. Toys were packed for distribution to the shelterers. Staff often carried out this work during their rest breaks and in their own time. [1998/36137]

Opposite below: Wood Green Underground station, December 1940. Up to seven tons of food was sorted, distributed and served to the shelterers each night. [1998/91182]

A canteen decorated for Christmas at King's Cross Underground station, 22 December 1944. A competition for the best decorated canteen was held amongst the stations. This entry came in the top three. [1998/20770]

Mrs Dorothy McKenzie, the first woman van driver to work for London Transport. Mrs McKenzie continued the work of the 'Timetable men', twelve of whom were called up to fight during the war. Duties included driving her van to check, change timetable bills, and if necessary replace any of the glass-panelled poster frames that advertised London Transport services. Formerly an ambulance driver, Mrs McKenzie averaged sixty miles a day in her van, travelling between Gravesend and Tunbridge Wells. [1998/35938]

Charing Cross Bill Store, 23 February 1943. Publicity advertising London Transport services was replaced by instructional and morale boosting posters. [1998/45980]

Putting the finishing touches to a stencilled sign at the Parsons Green Building Department, c.1940. [1998/36119]

Mrs I. Vance, a deputy chief tracer (left), and Mrs E. Clements, a clerk on staff records, act as enemy aircraft spotters on the roof of London Transport's Griffith House offices at Edgware Road, 19 May 1941. Staff offered their services for such work during their own time, outside normal working hours. [1998/48308]

A member of staff attends to a syphon recorder in an underground hydrophone recording room deep in South Kensington tube station, 22 June 1943. Hydrophones were placed on the bed of the River Thames to detect sounds from unexploded bombs. [1998/36463]

Above: Mrs Slater, a 'circuit installer's mate', aids a male colleague trackside at Uxbridge, 1 July 1942. As the war progressed, women increasingly began to take on work of a more skilled nature. On the railways, women helped to keep the system running safely and securely by maintaining the permanent way and signals. [1998/69402]

Right: 'Back Room Boys... They Also Serve – Cable Maintenance', by Fred Taylor, 1942. The shot above was used as a model for this poster. [1983/4/5573]

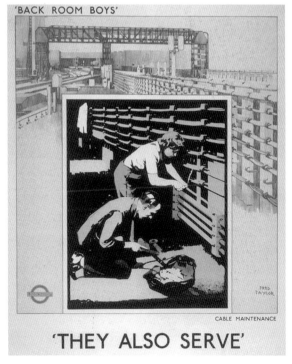

'BACK ROOM BOYS'

CABLE MAINTENANCE

'THEY ALSO SERVE'

Hot food is served to permanent way staff during a break from work, New Cross, 1 June 1943.
[1998/46800]

Right and below: Overhauling electro-pneumatic train stops and manufacturing components at the Signal Engineer's Department, Earl's Court, 29 July 1942. During the Second World War, almost 3,000 women were employed in London Transport's engineering departments. [1998/44186], [1998/36480]

Above and left: Mrs Bivins and Mrs Hill replace upholstery in an overhauled District line car; Mrs Hill can also be seen at the controls of an electric forklift truck stacking seats on to pallets at Acton Works, 13 August 1942. Rigorous maintenance of the railway track, signals and vehicles had to continue throughout the war. Regular inspection and overhaul of vehicles was carried out at Acton Works, which was set up in the 1920s to overhaul the trains on a production line basis. Cars were lifted from their bogies, stripped, repainted, and rebuilt. Interiors were washed, seats were vacuumed and replaced as necessary. [1998/35899], [1998/35900]

Opposite below: Mrs Sutton packs and lubricates the axle boxes of Underground cars, Acton Works, 13 August 1942. [1998/35907]

Above: Mrs Packer operates a rail tyre-reversing machine, Acton Works, 13 August 1942. Wages for women in engineering grades were equal to 90 per cent of the male rate, plus the women's war wage for the first six months of their service, rising to the full male rate plus the men's war wage thereafter. [1998/23485]

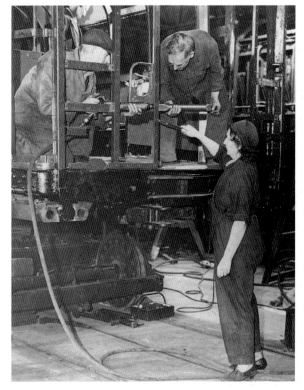

Above left: Mrs Cooper grinds an Underground car motor case down for re-stamping, Acton Works, 13 August 1942. [1998/35954]

Above right: Mrs Bullen operates a hammer driver while her male colleague assists, Acton Works, Smith's shop, 13 August 1942. For especially intricate work, skilled craftsmen (usually men) 'set the work' before handing over to female colleagues to complete the remainder of the job. [1998/91186]

Left: Mrs Gibbs and Mrs Houston heat and deliver rivets to two male colleagues carrying out repairs to an Underground car, Acton Works, 13 August 1942. Women carried out the majority of overhaul tasks excepting the heaviest manual work. [1998/35895]

Right: Making aluminium castings in the signal overhaul shop, Earl's Court, 29 July 1942. [1998/36074]

Below: Underground car overhaul continued on a reduced level during the war, but Acton Works was also used for non-transport war production such as munitions. Here, Mrs Crouch and Mrs Murray assemble details on bomb boxes, 13 August 1942. [1998/45835]

Fitter's assistants Mrs Maddren, Mrs Loller and Mrs Brixey assemble parts for tanks, Acton Works, 13 August 1942. [1998/35897]

Fitter's assistant Mrs Nicholl helps to assemble bogie trucks alongside fitter Mr F. Hockley, Acton Works, 13 August 1942. [1998/35901]

An audience of Acton Works staff are entertained by ENSA (Entertainments National Service Association) with a concert during an air raid, 16 August 1940. [2002/919]

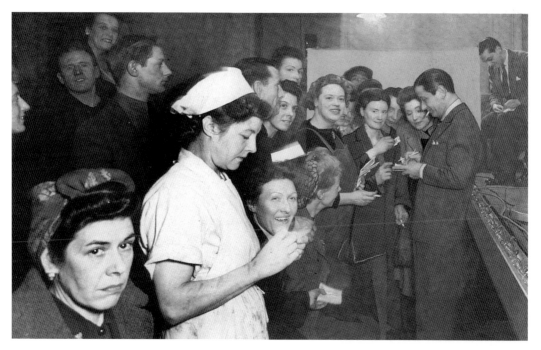

ENSA dinnertime entertainment for Charlton Works staff. Entertainer Geraldo (of 'Geraldo and his Orchestra' fame) signs autographs for members of staff after his 'Break for the Music' performance, broadcast by the BBC on 16 August 1940. [2004/8018]

BOILER MAINTENANCE

'THEY ALSO SERVE'

'Back Room Boys… They Also Serve – Boiler Maintenance', by Fred Taylor, 1942. Lots Road Power station in Chelsea generated electricity for the Underground, trams and trolleybuses. Women were employed there in many essential roles ranging from labourers through to engineering. [1983/4/5570]

Left: Labourer Mrs Turney pushes a wheelbarrow at Lots Road Power station, 29 June 1942. Work was often arduous, labour intensive and unusual for urban women at the time. [1998/35913]

Opposite above: Coal trimmer Miss G. Stanbridge shovels clinker or ash into a wheelbarrow, Lots Road Power station, 29 June 1942. [1998/71053]

Opposite below: Boiler cleaners Mrs Hainsbury and Mrs Smith examine and clean boilers, Lots Road Power station, 29 June 1942. [1998/35914]

 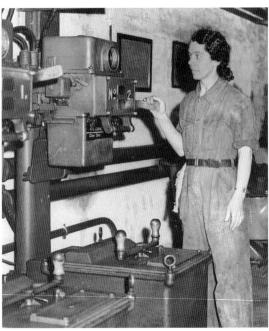

Above left: A stores woman sorts equipment into labelled pigeonholes, Lots Road Power station, 29 June 1942. [1998/46242]

Above right: Cap cleaner Mrs Burns, Lots Road Power station, 29 June 1942. [1998/35953]

Auxiliary plant assistant Mrs Bowen operates machinery, Neasden Power station, 1 July 1942. Neasden Power station was originally built by the Metropolitan Railway and was taken over by London Transport in 1933. [1998/68312]

Right: Mrs Golley paints steelwork at Neasden Power station, 1 July 1942. [1998/23590]

Below: Mrs Golley stops to chat with colleagues, Neasden Power station, 1 July 1942. War work not only provided women with an opportunity to work in jobs not previously offered to them, it also gave them the chance to widen their social circles. [1998/35928]

Opposite and above: Drill operators at Plessey's Underground factory, Redbridge, 1942. Plans to extend the Central line eastwards from Liverpool Street were postponed with the advent of war. A five-mile length of tunnel was offered as premises for a Plessey aircraft components factory, which was largely staffed by women in shifts of 2,000 workers, day and night. This was also known as Plessey Tunnel. A miniature railway was built to carry materials and completed parts to and from the workers. The Central line extension was finally opened through this tunnel after the war, in 1947. [1998/36009], [1998/83573], [1998/62211]

Land girls Mary Howe (formerly an art student) and Gwen Seale (formerly a General Post Office employee) cut 'Winningstadt' cabbages at London Transport's farm in Oak Field, Little Bushey, 8 September 1944. The London Passenger Transport Board had purchased large tracts of land for the extension of the Northern line, which was then subsequently postponed with the advent of the war. It was decided to put the land to good use to grow produce to supply the 135 canteens that served over 83,000 meals daily to its staff. All three farms sited are on land north of Edgware, bought for the planned tube extension to Bushey Heath, which was never completed. [2003/8723]

A Land Army girl plants potatoes at London Transport Gardens, Brockley Hill, 7 May 1941. [2003/8733]

London Transport farm at Brook Field, Bushey, 8 September 1944. Women's Land Army girl Rosie Pitteway gives refreshment to plough horse Blossom. [1998/62158]

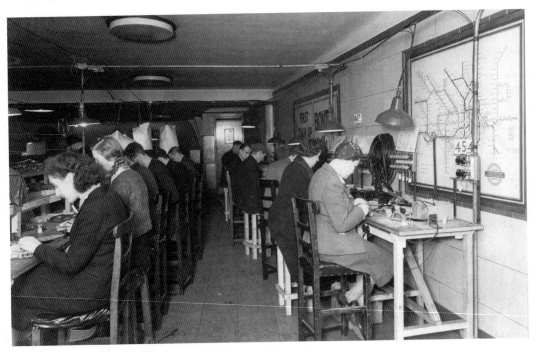

Above and below: London Transport's 'Spare Time' factory in a subway at Earl's Court Underground station, 17 January 1943. Staff worked in their evenings' spare time on war work, continuting £200,000 worth of free labour. [1998/23473], [1999/11196]

Trimming electrical wire to specified lengths, 1942. Over three hundred London Transport staff volunteered to make aircraft components in their spare time. The plan originated when a department was approached to do war work at the end of their ordinary duties; 160 volunteered at once. Staff performed the work quickly and proficiently and often with little training. The volunteers, representing many grades, from signal linemen to lorry drivers and from clerks to typists, provided over 1,000 extra hours of work a week. [2004/8036]

Here an assembly worker puts the finishing touches to a section of a Halifax at Leavesden Works, *c.*1941. London Transport joined forces with four motor companies to build over 700 Handley Page Halifax heavy bombers, using mainly female labour. [1998/84404]

A photograph shoot on the rooftop of 55 Broadway, showing the conductors and porters selected to attend a Victory Day procession on 8 June 1946. The ten women were chosen to represent all those who had made a contribution to the war effort during the Second World War. [2004/8294]

From left to right: conductors Irene Reed, Mabel Callaghan, Kathleen Leggott, and Ada Janes; porters Elizabeth Clarke and Elsie Birell; and conductors Dorothy Hunt, Kathleen Newman, Doris Roach and Lily Brooks. Elsie Birell was also a model for Eric Kennington's poster, entitled 'Seeing it Through – Station Woman, 1944'. [2004/8305]

" *How often, when I have talked with women engaged on*
every kind of job, sometimes a physically hard or dangerous
one — how often, when I admired their pluck, have I heard
them say, 'Oh, well, it's not much. I'm just doing my best
to help us win the war' "

Her Majesty the Queen broadcasting to the Women of the Empire
April 11, 1943

Her Majesty the Queen broadcasting to the women of the Empire, 11 April 1943. This was
one of a series of morale boosting wartime posters issued by London Transport.
[1983/4/10528]

four

1949–1978

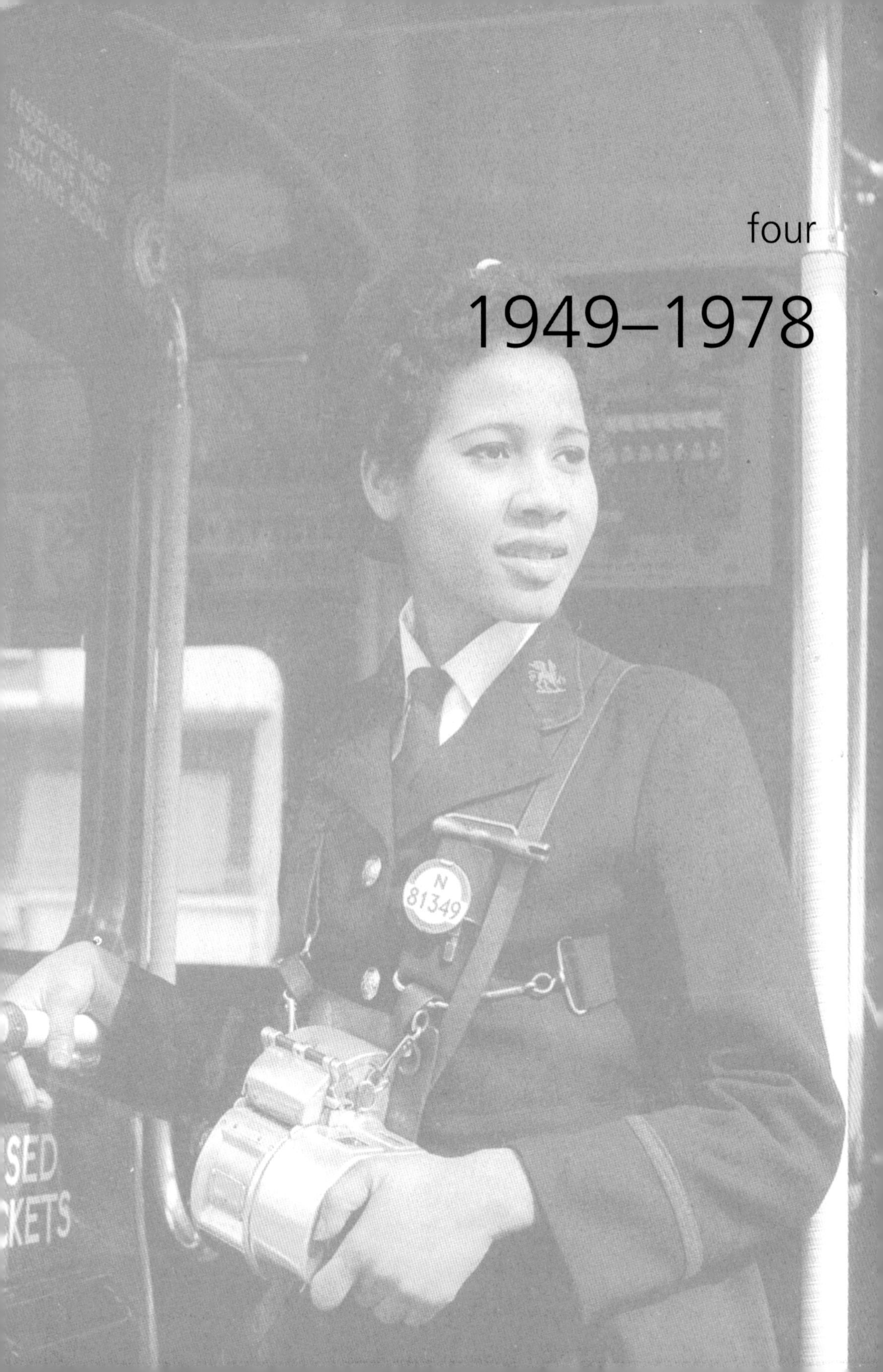

Left: Miss D. Drury operates a keypunch, central records office at 55 Broadway, 1949. The central records office was described in *London Transport Magazine* as being the 'nerve centre of all statistics about London Transport's staff'. Information pertaining to age, length of service and grade was recorded and reproduced on small rectangular cards (one per staff member). A small hole was punched in the card for each different item of information, and up to 960 different pieces of information could be recorded on each card. [1998/48790]

Right: Denese Drew from London Transport's purchasing office, who was a member of the junior staff club, posing for *London Transport Magazine*, Volume 4, No.10, in January 1951. Miss Drew was photographed at Baker Street Rifle Range, situated beneath the Underground station, for the cover of the staff magazine. The junior staff club was founded in 1949 and aimed to encourage under twenty-one year olds to take an active interest in sports and social activities. Under the guidance of London Transport's welfare office, members formed their own committee and ran all aspects of the club. Activities included classes in dancing, cookery, amateur dramatics and historical tours around London.

Right: London Transport Magazine, Volume 5, No.6, page 3, from September 1951. This was a page designed especially for London Transport's women staff. Pages often gave recipes, advertised patterns for making clothes, and displayed general advertisements and tips for hair and beauty products.

Opposite below: Miss E. Davies and Miss L. Stokely operate a Hollerith machine in the central records office, 55 Broadway, 1949. The machine sorted the punch-hole record cards at a rate of 400 a minute. The conception of a 'central records of staff statistics' office began prior to the Second World War, and was resurrected mid-1947. The office and machines used to collate staff information were considered pioneering at the time. The office produced valuable statistics for London Transport, whilst saving a great deal of monotonous clerical labour. [1998/48777]

Cashiers at work, using the 'Brandt automatic cashier', a mechanisation system used to make up wage packets, Treasurer's Department, 55 Broadway, 12 February 1956. [1998/48758]

Telephonists working the London Transport Head Office switchboard, 55 Broadway, April 1956. [1998/48334]

The Commercial Advertising department of the general office, 55 Broadway, 20 February 1957. [1998/55453]

Above left: Portrait shot of Miss Pitman, a clerk, sitting at a manual typewriter, 1957. [1998/47480]

Above right: The computer room, showing the huge early types of computers in use that held staff records, Baker Street Offices, 20 January 1971. [1998/85749]

Left: Miss Grace Cole works at a stitching machine in the book-folding and sewing section, Effra Road Printing Works, Brixton, March 1949. At the time of this photograph, Miss Cole had worked in the printing shop for twenty-two years. Many employees started work as young girls and remained there for years. [1998/49669]

Below: Seventeen year old June Ellenden sorts tickets, Effra Road Printing Works, Brixton, 1949. Jobs were interchangeable, and training was given by working on each stage of the printing process. [1998/49649]

Opposite below: Mrs Rose Bates packs ticket rolls as they come off of the production line, Effra Road Printing Works, Brixton, 1957. Newly wound paper rolls were mechanically punched, inspected, packed and sent on their way. [1998/54785

Above: Effra Road, Brixton, ticket office section, 1957. This photograph was taken to record recently installed equipment. More than eight million paper rolls a year were produced to supply the 14,000 Gibson roll ticket-issuing machines used by London Transport bus conductors. The Gibson machines had entirely replaced Bell Punch machines by this time. [1998/47508]

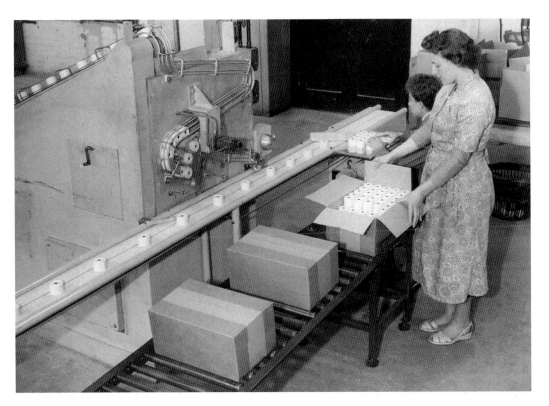

'Children's London', by Carol Barker, 1973. Barker designed posters for London Transport between 1966 and 1979. [1983/4/7914]

A tube stock interior from a 1938 train, with seating moquette designed by Enid Marx in 1949. Frank Pick approached Enid Marx to design seating fabrics for Underground trains in 1937. This design, known as the 'Shield' pattern, was used on re-upholstered vehicles on the Bakerloo, Northern and District lines. In the 1950s and 1960s Marx also designed posters for London Transport. [1998/89021]

Pastry cooks attend a practical lesson in the new Baker Street Canteen and Training School, 3 August 1949. The training centre was considered to be one of the first of its kind. It was run by an industrial organisation and allowed for a system of methodical training for both new entrants to the canteen service and those being upgraded. There were two main divisions; the general demonstration kitchen where cooks could learn how to prepare meat, and the pastry demonstration kitchen. [1998/47277]

Above. left: Croydon Food Production Centre, the 'Finishing Room', October 1950. A woman pastry cook finishes off jam tarts with cream in a tray destined for Hanwell Trolleybus Depot. [1998/85870]

Above right: Croydon Food Production Centre, the 'dispatch room', October 1950. The food production centre produced more than 350,000 cakes, buns and rolls for consumption in over eighty London Transport canteens all over London. [1998/48480]

London Transport requires

WOMEN CANTEEN ASSISTANTS

MINIMUM AGE 18 YEARS

Shift work — no all-night duty

STARTING RATE £4·10·6

Certain free travel facilities · free meals
Uniform (with laundry allowance) provided
Promotion prospects

Call or Write to

**The London Transport Recruitment Centre,
Griffith House, 280 Marylebone Road, N.W.I**
or ask for details at your local Employment Exchange

Above: 'London Transport Requires Women Canteen Assistants', 1954. [1983/4/11450]

Right: This portrait shot of a canteen assistant serving tea was used on a poster recruitment campaign for canteen staff in 1951. In the post-war years, London Transport suffered from staff shortages and began a series of recruitment campaigns overseas, in particular in Ireland and the Caribbean. Women were encouraged to apply for jobs as bus conductors, station staff and canteen assistants. [1998/47288]

Below: Staff relax in the lounge area of Windsor staff hostel, 7 July 1955. The hostel was run for London Transport by the YWCA (Young Women's Christian Association) particularly for female members of staff who had come to work in England for the first time. [1998/46599]

Opposite below: Kingston Bus garage canteen, servery area, 3 July 1950. [1998/47029]

Catering Instructor Mrs Bradford gives a lesson in oven cleaning to a group of catering trainees, Baker Street Training Centre, 10 July 1968. [1998/85733]

Merna Miller poses as London Transport Catering Queen, 1971. Merna was born in Jamaica; she joined London Transport in March 1970 as a catering assistant. [1998/18599]

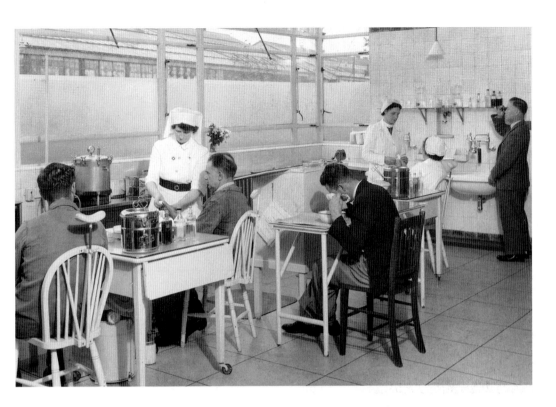

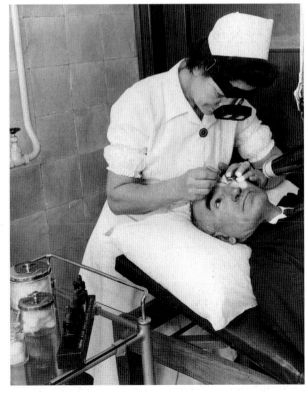

Above: Nurses attend to patients in the surgery at the Industrial Health Centre, Chiswick Works, January 1948. The surgeries, operated with qualified staff, were also situated at Acton, Charlton and Aldenham Works. Emergency and first-aid treatment was provided for work-related injuries and accidents or sickness. Some 10,000 staff members were covered in this way. [1998/40017]

Right: Sister Cotton attends to the eye of a male patient, Industrial Health Centre, Chiswick Works, 17 October 1963. Clinical examination of serving staff and new recruits accounted for two-thirds of the work of the medical departments. Various health schemes advised new and existing recruits on maintaining good health whilst working for the company. [1998/46082]

Left: 'London Transport Wants More Conductors Now', Clement Dane Studio, 1954. [1983/4/6693]

Below: Conductor Mrs E.M. Thurgar plays dominoes in the canteen with two colleagues, Hammersmith Depot, 30 July 1947. [1998/84126]

A posed shot of trolleybus conductors in the staff rest room, Fulwell Depot, 7 August 1947. [1998/47294]

Bus conductor Ms Harbour (badge number N39944), New Cross Garage, 1959. Ms Harbour's photograph featured in a recruitment poster, 'It's a good job... it's a service', 1959. [1998/84880]

Above left: Bus conductor Mrs McKenna, (N44681), October 1952. [1998/84752]

Above right: Bus conductor Miss Stella Henebury (N37131), Riverside Garage, December 1950. Miss Henebury's photograph featured in a recruitment poster 'Women Conductors Required', 1951. [1998/84950]

Above left: Bus conductor Sheila Fee (MM46118), Hendon Garage, 17 September 1959. [1998/84865]

Above right: Bus conductor Agatha Claudette Hart (N81349), Stockwell Bus Garage, 4 March 1962. [1998/86291]

Above left: Bus conductor Bowes (BB64184), Enfield Garage, 17 January 1963. Ms Bowes' photograph featured in recruitment poster, 'Conduct a London Bus', 1963. [1998/47559]

Above right: Bus conductor Mrs M. Sherlock, (N72707) New Cross Garage, 3 December 1965. [1998/86261]

Left: Bus conductor Mrs Barr (N89013), Cricklewood Garage, 23 May 1968. [1998/85457]

Store woman Mrs Violet Iredale fits Miss Linda Lamb, aged twenty-two, for a new uniform, London Transport Clothing Store, Acton, 23 July 1974. [1998/20548]

Pauline Bartley, a twenty-three year old conductor from Stockwell Garage, is crowned 'London Transport's Gala Charm Girl' by LT Chairman Kenneth Robinson at Osterley Sports Ground, 1977. Miss Bartley served on bus route 88, between Mitcham and Acton Green. A panel of judges that included the Mayor and Mayoress of Hounslow, Fulham FC manager Bobby Campbell and BBC Radio London personality Susie Barnes chose Ms Bartley from over sixty contestants at the annual pageant. London Transport continued its tradition of holding beauty competitions for female staff until the early 1980s. [1998/87213]

Right: 'Serving London…
Stationwomen', 1960.
[1983/4/7163]

Opposite: Jill Viner, London Transport's first woman bus driver, poses in the cab of an RT-type double-decker bus, June 1971. Formerly a conductor from Norbiton Garage, Jill was among the first women conductors to apply for driver training. She received twenty-four days of intensive training at Chiswick Training Centre before passing her Passenger Service Vehicle driving test. Her instructor Maurice Patchett (who doubled for Roger Moore in a stunt driving sequence for the James Bond film *Live and Let Die*) revealed Jill was a 'model trainee', who was 'quick to pick up things'. Jill faced a two-hour-long photo-call and press conference where reporters and cameramen covering the momentous occasion besieged her. [1998/83575]

Above and below: Newly appointed stationwomen are measured and issued with uniforms at Lambeth North Underground Clothing Store, December 1950. [1998/85804], [1998/84910]

Above and below: Stationwomen are instructed in the use of signals by miniature demonstration trains that run on electric tracks. The trainees also get used to hearing their own voices making announcements such as 'Mind the doors, please!' on a tape recording machine. Lambeth North Training School, December 1950. [1998/46299], [1998/46301]

Stationwoman Miss L. Bell signals on the station platform at Park Royal, Piccadilly line, 28 October 1949. Miss Bell also appeared in a recruitment poster, 'Stationmen and Women', by Hans Unger, 1951. [1998/47790]

Stationwoman Ms O. Hanson aids a passenger with an enquiry at Holborn station, 10 December 1965. [1998/47787]

Stationwoman Miss P. Eccleshall makes an announcement, Tower Hill station, 21 January 1969.
[1998/86171]

Above and left: Teams of tunnel cleaners known as 'fluffers' remove fluff and dirt from the tracks at Hyde Park Corner station, December 1955. If left to accumulate, the debris can severely disrupt the daily operation of the Underground system. The women worked at night during a period of four hours known as 'Engineering Hours', when all power to the tracks was switched off. [1998/86493], [1998/65711]

Above: Cleaning the bodywork of a surface stock car at Neasden Depot, 14 December 1954. [1998/51203]

Right: Travel enquiry staff in the recently opened enquiry booth in the booking hall of Piccadilly Circus station, May 1957. [1998/47659]

F igures in *'Expanding Horizons', Transport for London's Women's Action Plan 2004*, reported that women still only account for 22 per cent of TfL's workforce. Transport for London launched its first Women's Action Plan at the Mayor's fourth annual 'Capitalwomen conference' on 6 March 2004. Through research, analysis and talking to women of different ages, races, faiths and cultures, the plan attempts to expand the travel choices and improve the journey experiences of all women. One of the action areas of the plan aims to increase the number of women working for TfL through targeted recruitment and information events. Women will be encouraged to apply for posts in traditionally male areas of service, such as drivers and in engineering grades, as well as managerial roles. 'The ultimate goal for recruitment is to increase the number of women working for TfL in alignment with the London population (currently 52 per cent) at every level of the organisation from operational to senior management posts'.

Above: Hannah Dadds at the controls of a District line train, 1978. [1998/89884]

Opposite: Hannah Dadds, London Underground's first woman train operator, climbs into the cab of a District line train, 1978. Hannah joined London Transport in 1969 as a stationwoman, and qualified as a guard nine years later. In October 1978, she made history by becoming London Transport's first woman train driver. When Hannah's sister Edna became a guard the pair worked together for eighteen months, making history again as London Transport's first all-woman train crew. Edna also qualified as a train driver and the sisters continued working for London Transport until 1993. Hannah's achievement was recognised when she attended the Women Achievers' lunch at Buckingham Palace and met the Queen on 11 March 2004, the first women-only event of its kind to be held at the palace. [1998/89899]

Other local titles published by Tempus

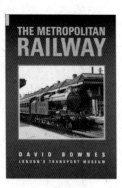

Metropolitan Railway
DAVID BOWNES

The Metropolitan Railway was the world's first underground railway, opened in 1863, and over the next twenty years –in partnership with the District Railway – it grew until there was an 'Inner Circle' of sub-surface railway, known as the Circle Line today. This book tells the story of this urban transport network and its importance in linking the city.

0 7524 3105 6

London's Railways
K.A. SCHOLEY

London's Railways gives a unique insight into the history of the railways in the Capital. This book brings the classic age of rail travel to life and demonstrates us just how much London was, and still is, dependent on the shimmering ribbons of steel that have penetrated both over and under the city from all directions.

0 7524 1605 7

The Willing Servant – A History of the Steam Locomotive
DAVID ROSS

Taking us through the last two hundred years, David Ross tells not just the story of the steam engine but also of its effects on mankind. From small beginnings, the railway locomotive was responsible for the speed of industrialisation in many countries, for commuting, for tourism, for industrial progress in all fields and for making the people of the world a transient workforce. Without it, the world would be a different place.

0 7524 2986 8

London – A Historical Companion
KENNETH PANTON

Kenneth Panton presents the characters, events, buildings and institutions that have shaped London over the millennia, from the Roman settlement to the cosmopolitan centre of culture and commerce it is today. In an accessible, comprehensive, illustrated dictionary format, this book can be used by armchair travellers and tourists alike.

0 7524 2577 3

If you are interested in purchasing other books published by Tempus, or in case you have difficulty finding any Tempus books in your local bookshop, you can also place orders directly through our website
www.tempus-publishing.com